CAMP MENDENHALL

CALIFORNIA JUVENILE DETENTION CAMP

Eric "Superman" Sturgess

Rose Of Sharon
PUBLISHING

ERIC "SUPERMAN" STURGESS

Printed Worldwide
First Printing 2025
First Edition 2025

10 9 8 7 6 5 4 3 2 1

Rose of Sharon Publishing books may be ordered through booksellers or by contacting:

Rose Of Sharon Publishing
roseofsharonpublishing.com
P.O. Box 186
Floresville, Texas 78114

ISBN: 978-1-967791-93-4 Paperback

Preface

I came across the photo album from Camp Mendenhall a few weeks ago. I figured it would be a shame for these people and their history to be forgotten. This album contains some fascinating photos. These pictures were taken in 1966 and are of excellent quality for that time period, considering the circumstances under which they were taken.

Camp Mendenhall had a photo club in 1966, and they would print out the pictures that the cadets took of themselves. Several last names are written under the photos in the cadets' album. The names: Clayton, Ford, Wilkerson, Daniels, Laster, Spratley, Cunningham, Jones, Dunham, and Calep.

I wonder what kind of lives the people pictured in this book lived? The youngest ones pictured were born in 1950. That would make them 75 years old in 2025. The majority of them have certainly passed on. I always find it strange to look at photos of people who have died. We live, we die, and life goes on. It's a cold fact of life. I find motivation in that to walk in integrity on the righteous path. The most significant accomplishment in life is to have those who know you the best respect you the most.

Looking at these pictures of these young men reminds me how fleeting our lives are. We are young and full of life one day, then, seemingly, we are middle-aged and burdened with infirmities and the realization that our lives are almost over. The Bible talks about the brevity of our lives here on earth: "What is your life? You are a mist that appears for a little while and then vanishes," James 4:14.

God bless you
Eric Sturgess
Romans 10:9-13.

Table of Contents

Introduction

Tucked away in the quiet hills of Lake Hughes stood two probation boot camps—Munz and Mendenhall—places designed not for military recruits, but for young offenders who had reached a breaking point. The teenagers who ended up here hadn't come to serve America; they had come to serve time. Each had crossed the line into drugs, gangs, and crime, and the county probation department was offering what might be their last chance: a few months of strict order, discipline, and a chance to reset their lives.

The program was straightforward yet demanding. At Camp Mendenhall, mornings began at 6 a.m. and ended at lights out by 8:30 p.m. In between, the young men cooked their meals, scrubbed their barracks, marched in drills, and attended accredited high school classes. They also sat in drug education seminars—places where some, for the first time, realized what those substances had been doing to their bodies and minds. Their time in camp could last three to six months, depending entirely on how they behaved.

Probation officers called it "discipline with dignity." There was no tearing down, no harsh drill-sergeant insults. The staff avoided profanity, focusing instead on respect. The belief was simple: drugs had already torn these teenagers down far enough. Now, order and structure could build them back up. Every "yes, sir" and every polished boot was meant to teach self-esteem, leadership, and responsibility.

The boys came from every corner of Los Angeles County. Some had been gang members since middle school. Some hadn't been to school in years. They carried tattoos, drug habits, and memories of street wars that felt impossible to escape. One sixteen-year-old admitted he had smoked PCP daily for three years before being arrested for armed robbery. Another confessed he loved his gang but knew it was leading him straight to prison. For many, dreaming about drugs was as real as the drills they performed each morning.

Life in Mendenhall was regimented, but it wasn't without glimpses of hope. A probation officer recalled a boy's face glowing when he realized he had finally earned enough credits to graduate high school. Others, during silent drills, admitted they thought about how they could change when they returned home. Certificates at the end of the drug education classes weren't just paper—they were proof that someone believed they could do more than survive the streets.

Still, everyone knew the real test began once they reached "the outs," as the inmates called life outside the camp gates. Old gangs would wait for them. Old temptations would call. Some were honest about their fears—afraid they might be too weak to resist. To help, probation officers stayed connected for six months after release and even worked with parents, many of whom had their own struggles with drugs or neglect. Families were invited to weekly education classes, learning alongside their sons how to break destructive cycles.

Change did not come easily. Some fought in camp and were sent back to court. Others, though, returned home showing responsibility for the first time in years. One mother whose son had just come home noticed the difference immediately: "He's acting responsible. He's going to school. I can count on him now." Her son's old gang came looking for him, but she stood firm at the door. "I let them know my son has changed," she said, "and I don't want them around anymore."

Camp Mendenhall wasn't a summer retreat. It was gritty, strict, and full of rules. Yet for those who took the lessons to heart, it became a rare turning point. In a place where their days were measured in drills and discipline, many learned—perhaps for the first time—that they could choose another path. Whether they would succeed beyond the gates was uncertain. But for a moment, within the structure of Mendenhall, they had been given a vision of what life could look like without gangs, drugs, or prison walls.

Photographs

About the Author

Eric has emerged as a highly accomplished investor and Day Trader, engaging in trading activities with a substantial value of stocks annually. He enjoys the status of a dedicated husband and father, being blessed with four wonderful daughters who hold a special place in his heart. Eric's existence revolves around upholding the virtues of a devout Christian, a devoted husband, and a caring father guided by the grace of God. His journey has been transformative, considering his challenging upbringing, and he now stands as an illustrious testament to the boundless possibilities achievable through faith in God.

Eric joined a criminal street gang as a teenager, and he was eventually arrested and put in a cage at the Long Beach City Jail. He dropped out of Jordan High School in Long Beach, California, in the 10th grade. Eric eventually got on the right path by the grace of God and obtained his GED the same month that he would have graduated. He joined the United States Coast Guard at 18, and after four years of faithful service, he was honorably discharged.

The following is an excerpt from his autobiography: "California Prison Confessions." "It was a typical beautiful summer night in Long Beach, California, and the three young teens fighting in the musty garage starkly contrasted the night's serenity. A teen called Bones was thrown against a wall, and a muscular teenager nicknamed E Double (me) rushed towards him and violently punched him in his lower back. Another youth named Tim Loc held Bones against the wall during this attack. E Double's knuckles landed with a thick-sounding thud as Bones grimaced and moaned in pain from each successive blow.

There's a look of pain and fear in Bone's eyes as E Double mercilessly lands blow after blow to his kidneys. E Double has spent years hitting the heavy bag in his garage, so his punches are devastating for his age. The beating lasted a minute, and the two teens stopped attacking the unfortunate victim. Amazingly, they all shook hands and embraced each other. We were all friends, and this was our modest gang initiation into our small clique called 'Six Feet Under.'"

Our tiny neighborhood gang in North Long Beach, California, had several members of various races: White, Black, and Hispanic. The definition of a criminal street gang according to the California Penal Code is as follows: "As used in this chapter, 'criminal street gang' means any ongoing organization, association, or group of three or more persons, whether formal or informal, having as one of its primary activities the commission of one or more of the criminal acts…having a common name or common identifying sign or symbol, and whose members individually or collectively engage in or have engaged in a pattern of criminal gang activity," California Penal Code 186.22(f).

Some of our associates committed serious crimes such as burglaries, drug sales, stealing cars, carrying guns, vandalism, and assaulting people. Although we were nothing but young punks, we were a criminal street gang according to the California Penal Code.

The FBI did a study entitled "Street-Gang Mentality: A Mosaic of Remorseless Violence and Relentless Loyalty." I want to quote a relevant part concerning young males who do not have a father or other positive male role models in their lives while growing up: "All gang members lacked male role models in their households, and when they lived with their mothers, they were rarely home because of work schedules. Gang members often lived temporarily with various people. All but one gang member reported that one or more immediate family members had a criminal history or abused drugs. Gangs attracted them because of their loyalty, stability, and sense of group identity."

There is an epidemic in this country of boys masquerading as men who don't take their responsibilities as fathers seriously. Many fathers aren't involved in their children's lives; if they are, they are a horrible example of what a real man should be. One of the main factors in young men ending up in the penal system is the lack of a father or, at the very least, a positive male role model when they were growing up. Absentee fathers are causing society to pay a high price for their selfish and callous actions.

Every day, I strive to be the best dad to the four beautiful daughters God has blessed me with. I live by the motto, "Be the man you needed as a child." I will not allow the actions of physically and emotionally abusive people to define who I am or hinder my advancement in life. You can choose to be bitter or better. I strive for excellence because living well is the best response to abusive people.

Eric Sturgess

God bless you and yours.

Romans 10:9-13

For those seeking to connect with Eric or gather additional insights about his upcoming projects, please visit his official website: EricSturgess.com.

Other Books

Prison Paños: Ink On Cloth

Prison Art Paños

Prison Art Hats

California Prisons:
Boxing Program History

Mini Prison Cells

California Prison Polaroids

Camp Mendenhall: California Juvenile Detention Camp

Imperial Japanese Military Photos 1937

Prison Art Envelopes

Prison Slang Dictionary